singing
a tree
into
dance

Jaki Shelton Green

Carolina Wren Press Poetry Chapbooks

Special Edition

Copyright 2003
CAROLINA WREN PRESS

The mission of the Carolina
Wren Press is to seek out,
nurture and promote literary
work by new and under-
represented writers, including
women and writers of color.

Series Editor:
David Kellogg

Design:
Anita Mills

Acknowledgements:

I am grateful to the Carolina Wren Press family and in particular I wish to acknowledge my gratitude to Andrea Selch, David Kellogg, and Anita Mills for their ongoing support, editorial expertise, artistic design vision, and strong determination to publish this chapbook in commemoration of my receiving the 2003 North Carolina Award in Literature. To all the ancestors, my mother and my "mama's people" I am forever indebted to you for the rich color of language that you gave to me as a child; to my warrior sister tribes and to my spirit brother tinker...axe' and thank you for always watching my back on and off the path; to Imani, Segun, and Eva, I am thankful for your unconditional love, patience, and the wonderment of being your mother.

—*Jaki Shelton Green*

Lifting Veils by Jaki Shelton Green, from **Poets for Peace**, copyright ©2002 by Timothy F. Crowley, with permission of The Chapel Hill Press, Inc.

This publication was made possible in part by generous grants from the North Carolina Arts Council. In addition, we gratefully acknowledge the ongoing support made possible through gifts to the Durham Arts Council's United Arts Fund.

Library of Congress Cataloging-in-Publication Data

Green, Jaki Shelton, 1953-
Singing a tree into dance : poems / Jaki Shelton Green.
p. cm. — (Carolina Wren Press poetry chapbooks, special edition)
Includes bibliographical references and index.
ISBN 0-932112-45-5
1. Feminist poetry, American. 2. African American women—Poetry. I.
Title. II. Carolina Wren Press poetry chapbooks
PS3557.R3723S56 2004
811'.54—dc22
2003027573

Contents

*for my husband, abdullateef,
who continues to stand with
me under dancing trees.*

rumors

what could the clouds be
whispering about me?
they don't even know my name

hush child!
hush

ain't i told you a thousand
times to whisper when we
walking thru the sky.

girl, cloud know your name
moon too
stars told 'em

they know 'bout you
know 'bout you before you were ever born

lifting veils

11 September 2001

i

it is a bloodstained horizon
whispering laa illaha il-lallah
prelude to a balmy evening
that envelops our embrace
we stand reaching across
sands, waters, airs full of blood

in the flash of a distant storm
i see you standing on another shore
torn hijab
billowing towards an unnamed wind.

we both wear veils
blood stained
tear stained
enshrouding separate truths.

ii

misty morning
teardrops of dust
choke and stain lips
that do not move
will not utter.
it is a morning of shores
sea shadows that caress memory
of another time
another veil
another woman needing
reaching
lifting

iii

into your eyes i swam
searching for veils
to lift
to wrap
to pierce
dance with
veils that elude such mornings
veils that stain such lips
veils tearing like music

iv

it is the covering of spirit
not the body
my hijab your hijab
connecting interweaving crawling snaking binding
into a sky that will not bend.

bring me your breasts

bring me your breasts
the ones hidden
inside pockets
under geraniums
covered with babies' breath
bring me your breasts
the ones that exploded
inside a lover's mouth
pushing a millennium of light
down a pulsating throat
bring me your breasts
so that i might stitch them to
the morning rain and weave
scarves with the needles of
their nipples
bring me your breasts
the melon ones
the pinecone ones
the ones jiggling with memory
the ones crying with relief
bring me the ones you have buried
the ones you have
shaped into bowls, cups, razors
bullets
bring me your breasts so the
dolphins might carry them to the
center of the sea
the center of the waterfall
the center of the storm
bring me the breasts you wore to
the dance, the breasts wet with potter's clay
bring me your breasts
i will build an altar
a sanctuary, a garden
i will soothe and oil and massage
memory back into them
teach them to long
teach them to dance
teach them to remember their names
their reasons, their seasons

bring me the breasts
i am building torpedoes
for their ride to the moon
i am building bird nests for those
that will remain piecing fabric
to skin, skin to leaf, skin to
tree
woman tree totem
bring me your breasts
i need the needles from your nipples
i need the blood for your thread
i need skin for this house

bring me your breasts
the ones crouching in kitchen corners
the ones belching out the blues
the ones that have forgotten the names
of the tunes they whisper
bring me the new born nipples
the ones with teeth
the ones whose eyes forget to close

bring me the breasts
the ones waiting for eclipses
the ones who count full moons
and run off to count clouds
the ones that ache and re-stitch
themselves to your face
bring me the lynched ones and the choked ones
the strapped ones and
the pierced ones
bring me the left ones
and the right ones
the ripe ones and the ones
longing to ripen
bring me the curled ones
the arched ones
the ones that have become knives
slicing the air
bring me the ones you
bathe in ginger
and lavender

the ones you soak in
rain water

bring me your breasts
the ones that need
and the ones that are needed
the ones that are cold
and the ones too hot to touch
bring me the ones that howl at
the moon
and the ones that will not speak
and the ones that speak in tongues
bring me your breasts
the flat ones, the round ones,
the lump ones, the red, yellow,
white, brown, and black ones
the ones stained and the
ones untouched
the ones photographed and
the ones uncovered
the ones veiled and the
ones drying in the wind
bring me the ones that are
awake and the ones too tired
to sleep
bring me the ones weeping
like willows and the ones
erect, sharp and full
of glass
bring me the silk ones
the linen ones
the cotton ones and
the wool ones
the ones bleached and the
ones unbleached
the breasts you wore to the
market and the breasts
you wore to church
i will build altars for these
sacrifices
i will build landscapes of your
healing

bring me your breasts
the mountains
the rivers
the paths
the gullies
bring me your geography
your rainforests and your sahara
i will navigate this map for you
with you, and because of you
i will strap this tornado of sinew,
muscle, bone, cartilage onto my
back and become the basket
so that you might heave,
stretch, contract back into your map
your geography

bring me your breasts
the coconuts
tomatoes
papayas
pears
mangos
of your youth
i will replant the seeds
snip your flowers
and sing sunshine into
your veins, your roots

bring me your breasts
the ones that reject water
and will only root
inside fire

bring me your breasts
the celluloid, runway
breasts
the cleavage that outruns
the rest of your body
bring them to this altar
bring me virgin breasts
bring me the ones that sleep alone
and the ones that have

multiplied themselves in the
birthing of snow, ice,
glaciers
bring the ones that hold fire
and kneel before crucifixes
the ones who veil their eyes
and the ones that draw curtains at noon

bring me your breasts
your theatre, your opera, ballet, breasts
your breasts of crayons
papier-mâché
your breasts of wire
string and rope
bring me your breasts
i will wrap them in tinsel and
create anthems for their
stage
bring me your breasts
the large ones, amazon warrior,
dangerous weapon, signals,
codes, secrets
bring me the small ones
cupped, hidden, dangerous
weapon, warrior codes and secrets
bring me the ones that
drink seawater, the ones
that harden to the
smiles of children, men, women
alike
bring me the breasts that laugh
and the ones that cry
the ones that scream
and the ones that whisper
the ones that crawl and
the ones that run

bring me your breasts
i will place them at the altar
between sonnet and verse
between sways and bends

i will grow flowers
in their valleys and fertilize
them with honey

bring me your breasts
i will hold them to mothers
sisters daughters granddaughters
grandmothers aunts
cousins lovers friends
i will hold them in bowls
calabashes, baskets, hats
urns, boxes, palms, wombs
cups, pockets, drawers, nets, bottles, tombs
skies, oceans

i will hold them in my mouth and hear them speak
of childhood girlhood womanhood motherhood loverhood
i will hold them in my womb so they might sprout
daughters sisters mothers to count the veins
we are holding these breasts in the captive light of morning
and the crystallized light of night
we become these breasts as we count ourselves back
into ourselves. our numbers our ages.
the weight of our tears
the height of our laughter
the width of our rebirthing

bring me the breasts
i will create a caravan
paint them
teach them the walk of the gypsy
the twirls of the dervish
the praises of the goddesses
the tricks of the shaman
the balance of the sky diver

bring me the breasts
i will teach them to moon walk
and teach them to write
we will write new songs
sitting on new moons

raising our skirts to the
crying mouth of a sky
that will not dry
i will keep the breasts near
and only touch them with
the feathers of the crow
only kiss them with the
lips of the crone

bring me your breasts
oh my mothers my sisters
my daughters my grandmothers
my lovers my friends
i will fold them and
help you tuck them
back inside, help you clear a field
and clean the ground for their
planting
bring me your breasts
the ones of amethyst, crystal, amber, and turquoise
i will soak them in my riverbeds
and dry them under the chinaberry
tree
bring me your cedar, mahogany
and brazillian breasts
your breasts of
teak and tortoise and marble and
clay
bring me your face, your feet
your hair and your nails
we will chase away the shadows as we
reinvent

bring me all your breasts
the ones with seeds, the ones with
bulbs, the ones with leaves, the
prickly ones, the sticky ones, the ones
growing weeds and the ones pruned and cultured
bring me the wild ones
the breasts that dress up in ribbons, purples
reds, velvet, and wear the smell of musk between their valleys
bring me the morning time

prayer time breasts, alongside the
peachy laced breasts of a saturday night fling
bring me your breasts
sisters of the circle
mothers of the yam
daughters of the shadows
bring them into the circles
bring them into the lodges
the houses the canoes the caves
the igloos the huts the holes the
attics the basements
bring them to me
bring them to your daughters
your mothers your granddaughters
your sisters
your aunts your grandmothers
your cousins your lovers your
friends

bring us the breasts so that
we might make ourselves over
and over again into the songs,
the dances, the poetry
the stories, the jewelry, the masks,
the curtains of our new selves

i go into rooms with rumi

i wear new faces into rooms
i've never gone into before; faces
stitched by hands of grandmothers
whose skin is clay
whose clan is wind
awakening from earth's sleep

i wear new faces into a
pitch of circles
a sky of dervishes
a dance of holy

i sit with river tears
that have stained the throats of elders
burned the soles of
wandering infants
and laced the tea of thirsty virgins

i sit with the wide leaves of palm trees
leaves hurled from the recesses
of their color, their markings
i wear new faces into rooms
where i've never gone before

i wear new faces
crawling into southern veins
screaming veins
flowing into southern creeks
alongside rail tracks choking with wisteria
tracks that refuse
to give back black bones
to black mothers
whose son's skin is now the fabric of steel

we wash kinky babies in dew drops
gathered in secret
muscadine smells

send trails of rapture and salvation
into woods
full of hushed song

juneteenth hugging and dancing
reclaim bootlegging warriors
reclaim hootchie kootchie damsels
straightening their backs
while stretching their legs
clad with red fox
primrose pomade
starched mouths
rinsing out red clay stains
for a baptism that will not cleanse

who will be the messenger of this land

who will be the messenger of this land
count its veins
speak through the veins
translate the language of water
navigate the heels of lineage
who will carry this land in parcels
paper, linen, burlap
who will weep when it bleeds
and hardens
forgets to birth itself

who will be the messenger of this land
wrapping its stories carefully
in patois of creole, irish,
gullah, twe, tuscarora
stripping its trees for tea
and pleasure
who will help this land to
remember its birthdays, baptisms
weddings, funerals, its rituals
denials, disappointments,
and sacrifices

who will be the messengers
of this land
harvesting its truths
bearing unleavened bread
burying mutilated crops beneath
its breasts

who will remember
to unbury the unborn seeds
that arrived
in captivity
shackled, folded
bent, layered in its
bowels

we are these messengers
with singing hoes
and dancing plows
with fingers that snap
beans, arms that
raise corn, feet that
cover the dew falling from
okra, beans, tomatoes

we are these messengers
whose ears alone choose
which spices
whose eyes alone name
basil, nutmeg, fennel, ginger, cardamom,
sassafras
whose tongues alone carry
hemlock, blood root, valerian, damiana,
st. john's wort
these roots that contain
its pleasures its languages its secrets

we are the messengers
new messengers
arriving as mutations of ourselves
we are these messengers
blue breath
red hands
singing a tree into dance

sonic collage/dying in a foreign country

i want to crawl into the grave
nibble along the wooden box
i want to nibble until my breath
becomes pinewood
i want to release you
into the cool smell of dark
touch your lips with my eyes
shudder when you awake

    i pour the wine
    sweep the ashes
    sift the wind's curse
    into bread loaves
    i pour the wine
    dry midnight tears
    stitch morning back into your eyes

        i pour the wine
        melt the glaciers forming in the fields
        scatter ashes
        rename daughters

daughters be the threshold of forbidden awakenings

i wrap my eyelids inside the feathers of day old birds
i watch for the sprinkling of sun rain
winter grows inside my mouth

    thighs hips
        your hip bone
            connected to my ...
                oh no ... what bone

daughters dream fields of lavender
dream about whispering tornados
i be riding hip bones
sucking whale bones

shadows of beds chairs strangers
hurl through the cyclone

are we in morocco

i taste coriander
i am weeping egyptian licorice
these blues
these ambers
these saffrons
these curtains
these veils
these portals
these footsteps

are we in morocco

Allahu Akbar
i smell the prophet's blood
inside this windstorm
a saharan tease
a nile thirst

      you woman one
         river stone thief
               hostage to thunderstorms
                    ju ju rain
                        you woman tree
                              roots
                              boiling
                              blood
                              slave
                              carnage
                      you woman snake
                              licking
                              crevices
                              searching
                              indigo
                              flesh

woman spirit
holding sky crumbs
stealing
chlorophyll
from the night

i

woman sprout
woman dirt
woman flood
woman hair

ii

wrap your woman stones
inside the feathers
of castrated cocks

iii

wrap your woman honey
inside plantain leaves

iv

wrap your bones
inside the bear's coat

v

woman cloud
weeping flute songs
weeping flute dust

vi

wrap your woman child
inside tornados

lavender
bronze
tremor red

vii

hold onto your hair
hold onto your nails
hold onto your skin
your juice
your spirit dirt
hold onto your windows
your doors
hold onto your male children
i eat them
i paint them
i write them
i rename
redress
reposition them

viii

      i am ready
        i am the thursday night in brazil
           wednesday morning in monks corner
          rehearsing
            high priestess
           litany
              i am ready
                red magic feet

           i am bronze
        blue
           female
                ready

ix

i am the last morning
in the barn
sweeping
old dust
old memory
old worn out story
into worn out corners
          i am skirts waiting to be danced
              i am ready
                  i am veils
                     ready to be lifted

x

i am the last night in the barn
candles
honey
penobscott fog
poems crawling from under the bed
poems falling off shelves
poems rolling from under rugs

were we in morocco

xi

i taste coriander
smell ginger in her hair

xii

poems lifted blankets, quilts, pillows
masquerading as sleep
poems spread open curtains
poems painted themselves on my lips
poems braided my hair

with the hands of my mother
poems oiled my feet
poems hennaed my thighs
poems crushed thunder chips
all over my lips
poems started licking my eyes
poems started caressing my face
poems measured my tears
that last night in the barn

xiii

in the barn
poems amputated your face
replaced your smell
your walk
your words

xiv

morocco is always here

i taste coriander
i smell ginger in your hair
my face is the shadow of all the poems
uncoiling
reaching
braiding
hip bone
to face

conjuring

i

bring me a crow's beak
four skins from four ribbon snakes
three day old robin's eggs
nine inches of black thread

eyes to blood filled cups
shoulder to parched lips
the angel drank all that your hands offered

ii

soak your keys to the house
in rose water

i will not ever sleep again without your words
guarding my bed

iii

soak his keys to the house
in camphor oil

your face aflame with birth
dropped seeds from pillow to pillow

iv

place all keys in a blue handkerchief

it is the light in the east calling my name

v

prick your third finger on your left hand

we stop sweating long enough
to remember to rename ourselves

vi

apply blood to four corners of blue handkerchief

earth angels disguise themselves as virgins

vii

fold
bury blue handkerchief
under his mother's doorstep

you present me earth for the flowers
for the midwifery of full moons
and seasonal eclipses

viii

wash your feet before entering any room in your house

make me come on the edges of your poems

ix

plant violets inside his trumpet

i become ink
permanent inscription
on be-bop memory

x

cook rice before sunset

staccato of stains in motion
a color we could not name

xi

raise your naked feet to the ceiling

bruised melodies swallow a storm of fire
as earth angels grow wings

visitations

i

there is a lizard in my throat
it's been there since I was two
when i became thirty
and then for nine more years
it tried and tried to come out

only the clear oval eyeless fish
swimming on the bottom of my ocean floor
sing songs that convince
the lizard to wait
wait until she's fifty, she'll pull
the stopper
we'll all rush out

ii

tonight is a time without sky
my son travels against dark light
i am convinced that a wiser
woman
an older woman with razors
inside her womb's gate
feeds him
ground snakes wasps nectar from
her breast

iii

this is a living room formed
by my hands
i sit alone surrounded
by eucalyptus, benin masks,
masks with golden eyes, pictures
of all the ones who made
me who i am
pictures of all the ones who tell me my
name is granddaughter
plants whose leaves resemble

tongues, amber crystal, soapstone eggs,
shells that rattle with sea music,
turkish rings, kente cloth,
symbols of woman, daughter, mother
lover
symbols of funerals, weddings, gardens
symbols of daybreaks that look the
same as dusks

iv

there was a lover who watched the
lights change in my eyes
who counted my braids
mailed me pieces of the sun inside
envelopes that smelled like
cornfields, burned leaves
drying seaweed

v

there was a lover who used to
kiss my toes
tongue trailing the broadness
of my feet
before I painted them with
the sweat of hemlock

vi

there was a lover who swam
with the dolphins
snorkeled, presented me jewels
from the nile, from the waters
of the atlanta, from the creeks
of virgina
a lover who played music
backwards on the flutes belonging to
yemassee grandfathers

vii

there is a wiser woman
whose lips
hold my son until the night
rips back its covers

viii

there are men i have loved
men i want to love
men i will never love
men i must love
men i cannot love
men i will love
men i will remember to forget
to love
but no man will make me smear honey
on his picture holding nine pins
between my eye sockets
no man will make me
present offerings to obatala
or cross my grandmother's grave
or wear white dresses for nine mornings
wear white beads, burn white candles
no more men will or can force
me to stand in the eye of firestorms
seducing the flames that lick at my
name

ix

no more men will i forget
their names or the names of their seed
no more men to cause me to speak
to the light in new languages that
singe the back of my tongue
no more men will cut slices
in my tongue as their gods will me to
speak through this woman house
no more men will open
the doors to my breasts

no more men will i count their footsteps
leaving my bed
no more men will i swim tired bloody
holding their weapons in between my teeth
no more men will i give away to this venus
catcher inside my womb swallowing
their heads leaving me torsos
for my art

x

they will say
you are an angry bitch
they will say you are a woman
scorned
they will say
you need a good fucking
i will say damn straight
i am woman who is alive inside words
that turn silver at the edges
alive in a world of blues and whites
alive inside the head of the man
in her head
in her bed
alive in the living room having
left the man alone asleep
in her bed
she goes to write a poem
wait on her son listen to rain
kill an ant that's much too
black for the whiteness of her
curtains

xi

i will remember the other men whose
faces become borders for newly
painted other rooms other colors